CW00402776

Dear Max

We loved your article about squirrels and thought that this second-hand book would inspire you further! There were red squirrels to be seen on the Isle of Wight — we were privileged to catch sight of them during our stay there for 6 years.

With love from the Miller family

# THE RED SQUIRREL

First published in 2017 by SCOTLAND: The Big Picture
www.scotlandbigpicture.com

All rights reserved.

Words by Polly Pullar and Neil McIntyre.
Images by Neil McIntyre except those listed below:
James Shooter : P28, P30/31, P120/121
Peter Cairns : P117
Jackie Walker : P10

Project management by Peter Cairns, Mark Hamblin & Emma Brown : www.scotlandbigpicture.com
Promotional film produced by James Shooter : www.scotlandbigpicture.com
Book design by Louise Jones & Adam Alexander : www.cairngormfutures.co.uk
Illustrations by Angus Grant : www.angusgrantart.com
Text editing by Richard Bunting : www.richardbunting.com
Book production by David Brimble : www.davidbrimble.com
Colour reproduction by DawkinsColour Ltd : www.dawkinscolour.co.uk
Printed and bound in Italy by Printer Trento : www.printertrento.it

The Forest Stewardship Council ® (FSC) is an independent, not for profit, non-government organization established to support environmentally appropriate, socially beneficial, and economically viable management of the world's forests.

This book is made with paper from responsible sources and meets the eligibility requirements stipulated by the FSC.

FSC
www.fsc.org
MIX
Paper from
responsible sources
FSC® C015829

ISBN: 978-0-9568423-1-2

10 9 8 7 6 5 4 3 2 1

A catalogue record of this book is available from the British Library.

No part of this book may be used or reproduced in any manner without written permission from the publisher, except in the context of reviews.

# Contents

# SCOTLAND
## THE BIG PICTURE

Amplifying the case for a wilder Scotland.

It wasn't so long ago that a rich, wild forest stretched its fingers across much of the Scottish Highlands. Beavers and cranes found sanctuary in shaded wetlands, wild boar foraged in open glades and lynx stalked the forest edge. Above in the canopy, red squirrels scurried and scolded, travelling wooded highways that extended from one horizon to the next.

Today less than 2% of that forest remains. Scattered across the landscape in isolated fragments, these islands of trees still support many of Scotland's most celebrated wildlife characters – capercaillie, pine martens, wildcats and of course, red squirrels. Banished from much of Britain by hunting, habitat loss and more latterly, competition from the introduced North American grey squirrel, the red holds on in Scotland, now very much its British stronghold. Its future however, is inextricably linked to the forest on which it depends.

Huge swathes of the Scottish Highlands remain bare, stripped of the woodland which once supported a complex web of life. It may never be possible to recreate the ecological jigsaw of the past but a richer, more vibrant wooded landscape can return, providing niches for a diverse array of species as well as improving soil quality, absorbing water and helping regulate our climate.

Expanding and joining up the wild forest will bring a wealth of ecological and social benefits. It will also help red squirrels, providing them with corridors along which they can return to parts of Scotland where they've not been seen for centuries.

This book showcases what is undoubtedly one of Britain's best-loved mammals and we're delighted to be working with Neil McIntyre and Polly Pullar to shine a light on the red squirrel and its forest home. Beyond that however, the book is a rallying call. Trying to save one species in isolation really doesn't make sense even if we had all the time in the world, and we most certainly do not. If we're serious about reds expanding their range, we have to get on with the business of restoring a wild forest network and allowing natural processes to nurture a dynamic community of inter-dependent organisms, red squirrels included.

**Build it and they will come.**

# THE RED SQUIRREL

## A FUTURE IN THE FOREST

Images: Neil McIntyre
Words: Polly Pullar

# The Red Squirrel: A Future in the Forest

## Introduction by Neil McIntyre

**W**hat is it about this intriguing little creature that captures the hearts of so many people? Sometimes that can be hard to define. My very first memories of seeing a red squirrel when I was a small boy are now vague, yet those fleeting glimpses ignited a passion that burns bright to this day.

When my father moved to a new job near Aviemore, in what is now the Cairngorms National Park, sightings became more regular as this is red squirrel heartland. Living over a mile from the main road, I had to cycle each morning to catch the school bus and it was during this daily commute along a wooded lane that I would catch a glimpse of a red flash – or occasionally, a closer, more prolonged view as a squirrel peeped around a tree, almost teasing me into a challenge to find out more. I grew accustomed to these exchanges and started to spend time watching their mischievous antics, sometimes becoming so absorbed I missed the school bus – well worth it in my opinion! As the years rolled by, my interest in red squirrels grew and slowly morphed into something of an addiction.

In early adulthood, my passion for wildlife photography began to emerge, and my thoughts immediately turned to the cheeky, charismatic small creature I had grown to love. I wanted to share with others my encounters with this forest sprite and my camera unlocked the door to their secret lives. It quickly became apparent, however, that whilst relying on chance encounters in the forest was

fine for squirrel observation, it was pretty useless for achieving the in-depth images I was hoping for. After a few months I had only a handful of mediocre pictures to show for my efforts. I needed a new approach – and although it now seems completely obvious, I started to try and bring the squirrels to me. Food was clearly the answer. I chose a mixed woodland site just a couple of hundred metres from home. With a glorious array of beech, oak and Scots pine, I could see the possibilities were endless, if only I could lure the squirrels to this spot.

By the end of day one, the food lay untouched. It was the same on day two. Then on day three every single hazelnut that I'd put out had vanished. Was it squirrels, or was it wood mice? I just couldn't tell, as there were no shells left to examine. The next day a shell had been discarded onto a nearby beech stump. It was broken in half without a gnawed hole, the tell-tale sign of a mouse or vole. This was the work of a red squirrel and I literally jumped with joy. Could this be the beginning? That same afternoon I popped up a portable hide, and the next morning returned full of eager anticipation. I put out the food and entered the hide expecting a long wait. After just half an hour, I heard the distinctive scratching of a squirrel's claws gripping a tree trunk as it descended to the ground. I could tell the squirrel was on the pine immediately behind my hide but then, in a flash, it was right in front of my camera, as it sat breaking a nut on an old decaying stump. I hardly dared breathe – but as the first squirrel relaxed, it was joined by another, and an hour later I had witnessed more red squirrel activity than in all the years I'd been watching them.

All this happened back in 1991. Now, many generations of red squirrels later, they still thrive in my local woods, and the daily feeding ritual continues. Over the years they have become so accustomed to me that I no longer need a hide. I can now move about without them reacting, almost becoming part of their secret world – and it is this level of acceptance, even trust, that has allowed me to capture the images in this book. My intention over all these years has not necessarily been to reveal every facet of squirrel behaviour, but to capture their individual spirit and character. And – crucially – to show the connection between the squirrels and the woodland on which they depend.

A stroll through an old Caledonian pine forest fragment, amongst sturdy trunks and chaotic gnarled branches, where a red squirrel might scamper or sit motionless, tucked close to the mighty frame of an old granny pine, is an experience I never tire of. But these unique forests are now small, isolated and in some cases, dying. There is finally a will to expand and link these islands of woodland and to allow red squirrels to return by themselves to their former strongholds. More native woodland and more red squirrels is surely something worth striving for?

I am very lucky to have squirrels as my neighbours and it is my hope that this book will bring you a sense of their personality, so that you too can feel a part of some of the special moments I have witnessed. What is it about red squirrels? They have become part of my everyday life and I would be lost without them. But – perhaps more than that – red squirrels and the forests in which they make their home represent what it is to be wild and free. What better way is there to live?

# Introduction

The glorious red squirrel has fascinated me for as long as I can remember, but over the past 20 years, through a series of close encounters, I think I have come to know it a little better. I consider myself fortunate indeed to have red squirrels living in close proximity to my home – yet the more I watch and study this lovely mammal, the more I realise how much there is to learn.

I am honoured to be providing text to accompany Neil McIntyre's world-class images. An outstanding, award-winning wildlife photographer, he has spent much of his adult life dedicated to recording the lives of squirrels in a stronghold in the ancient pine forests surrounding his Cairngorm home. His astonishing pictures portray his passion, revealing the rewards of thousands of hours spent waiting for that perfect pose, unveiling as never before the intimacies of a red squirrel's world.

Neil has captured the secrets of his squirrels and their forest home in every season. A rampant game of prenuptial tig around a wind-sculpted tree that has withstood the elements for over a century; a shaft of brilliance piercing fresh new leaves, etching the auburn coat and silken-blonde ear tufts of his subjects with pure gold; crystalline raindrops backlit on a web; a roe buck in dappled sunlight framed by birch trunks; the rare twinflower and a tracery of grey-green lichens dripping from spidery boughs; the silhouette of a crested tit against the apricot blur of gloaming. These are but a few of the vignettes that are characteristic of Neil's work as he incorporates minute details of the living breath of the forest fauna and flora.

Neil's images also brim with humour. Above all, they capture that elf-like spirit that is so integral to the aura embracing the red squirrel. He shows the squirrels' lithe and agile little bodies, leaping at full stretch - flying squirrels in the depths of Scottish woodland where you can scent the leaf litter, and the intoxicating aroma of pine resin. Amid visions of that beautiful little face peeping mischievously around a trunk, or peering down on an imposter whilst crossly signalling with its expressive tail, Neil's photographs tell a story and highlight the importance of nurturing the wild. Moreover, they highlight that fragility and how much we stand to lose if we do not sit up and take note. Now.

# Squirrel central

Living in Highland Perthshire, another of the red squirrel's strongholds, I have viewed at first hand the remarkable results achieved by providing suitable habitat. Just 17 years ago I seldom saw these flashes of brilliance in the immediate area. Now – having planted some 5,000 suitable native trees on our small south-facing farm – I bear witness to what can be achieved on even a minute scale, and excitingly in a relatively short time frame. When Neil first visited, he called it 'Squirrel central', as squirrels raced around in the trees opposite the kitchen window, and rushed about the garden busy burying winter stores. The squirrels are here breeding in dreys that we can see from the house, delighting us with their daily presence, infecting us with their spirited joy. And we are ecstatic to have them. Even washing-up becomes a pleasure with a view such as this. Forest acrobats – Nature's trapeze artists hurrying from tree to tree.

However, we cannot afford to become complacent – for the red squirrel still teeters on the brink, and continues to need our help, now more than ever. We must seek to open new branches by foresting for its future so that it may safely spread, travelling through linked woodland highways moving from drey to drey, and returning to its previous strongholds. It is our hope that as you savour these outstanding images, you will understand why time is of the essence.

Red squirrel country. The rich, vibrant forest, which once stretched across much of the Highlands is now confined to isolated fragments, preventing red squirrels from recolonising former haunts.

# The Forest Sprite

Some images take weeks of planning; some take months. On rare occasions, however, the most pleasing images happen out of the blue. Such was the case with this – possibly my personal favourite squirrel image.

I was out with a workshop client and after a few minutes of setting up, I realised I had forgotten my spare camera battery. With no squirrels in sight, I sneaked back to the car – but on my return decided to approach from a different angle, so as not to disturb any approaching squirrels.

Immediately I was struck by how different the forest looked from this approach. The tall pines appeared even more imposing – and as I admired them, a squirrel suddenly emerged from behind a majestic pine trunk and stood proudly on its meandering roots. Though the mighty tree dwarfed the diminutive squirrel, they looked so perfectly connected, interdependent. I knew instantly this was a scene that told many stories; a picture like this should need no words.

I took a few tentative steps to one side to optimise the framing, imploring the squirrel not to move. Thankfully I was a good distance back and the squirrel was totally unaware of my presence, instead intent on studying my client who remained at the original spot.

After a minute or so, the little squirrel had satisfied itself that all was well and went on its way. Forgetting the battery for once proved to be fortuitous – and changing my return route turned this into a stroke of real luck. I could never have planned such a shot. For once, this is a picture that happened through sheer chance.

# A beginning - early colonisers

The red squirrel has been in the British Isles for over 10,000 years. It arrived after the end of the last Ice Age, but has been up against strong odds ever since. Like many of our creatures, it has had to learn to live with a continuous forest ebb and flow – high tides when pioneer species grew in abundance, and trees began a steady unimpeded march covering the landscape with a lush, verdant blanket, and conversely dramatic low tides, as they dwindled to near non-existence.

Though natural forces, including changes in climate, have played a part, it is man who is largely responsible for the loss of Scotland's great boreal forests that once sprawled freely, painting the landscape with a richness now seldom seen. Dominated by Scots pine, oak, birch, aspen, juniper and rowan, this diverse, interconnected ecosystem is crucial to a host of species including such specialists as the red squirrel, capercaillie, Scottish crossbill, and rare crested tit, and previously included wolf, beaver, bear, moose, wild boar and lynx amongst its noble creatures. The beavers are now back – but what of the others?

The British Isles has a long history of deforestation. Since Neolithic times trees have been felled in vast number. By the 15th century – largely due to habitat depredation – the red squirrel had disappeared from Ireland altogether, whilst acute timber shortages in the 15th and 16th centuries and further felling led to a near extirpation of squirrels in Scotland too.

At the same time the mighty capercaillie – our largest, most impressive member of the grouse family – disappeared altogether, and later – during the 1830s – had to be reintroduced to Scotland from Scandinavia.

Tragically some forests were burned in a bid to eradicate the perceived wickedness of the wolf that clung on tenaciously until the 18th century, and woodland was also torched during battles.

Capercaillie, an emblem of the northern pinewood.

The swift development of agriculture – that began with early settlers growing meagre crops, and keeping half a dozen animals for their own needs – eventually led to massive tracts of forest falling to clear-felling projects, making way for a new agricultural vision, and still continues with everyday habitat loss. Add to this a past demand for timber for shipbuilding, and several major war efforts, the Industrial Revolution, and an explosion in the human population, and it's not difficult to understand how our primeval woodland diminished.

The arrival of sheep and a major rise in deer numbers added over-grazing pressures to an already beleaguered landscape. This in turn halted any hope of natural regeneration. Man in his ignorance has seldom thought of the bigger picture; the wild wood is the framework on which the health of the entire ecosystem hangs. It has but a toehold, like so many of its unique creatures.

Today native woodland covers only two per cent of Scotland's land mass. This paucity of habitat is to the detriment of all living species, including man. For the red squirrel, many forests have become marooned islands where the population remains static – or worse still, dwindles altogether. It was once said that in many parts of Scotland, a squirrel could widely travel in any direction without ever touching the ground. That vision has long gone.

# Centuries
of history

On the positive front, we are becoming enlightened, and finally understand the need for healthy native forests with trees of all ages. Many charities and conservation bodies, as well as private landowners, are working hard to restore and replant to provide a rich forest network, particularly in places where trees previously cloaked remote glens and spread far into crags, ever on towards the snow-line.

Examples of beautiful remnants of the ancient Caledonian Forest – that include Rothiemurchus, Glen Affric, Glen Lyon, Glen Feshie, Glen Tanar, Glen Moriston, Glen Strathfarrar, Abernethy, the Black Wood of Rannoch, and Loch Maree – are recognised as some of Scotland's finest assets. And it is the image of a mature, wind-honed Scots pine that is so often seen on card and calendar to portray Scotland. Yet how many people know that this ancient Caledonian pinewood, and the species dependent on it, is now at the very end of its life? It is possible that some of these gnarled granny pines have witnessed centuries of history, and with it perhaps extraordinary changes in human attitudes towards ecology.

# The squirrel hunt

I t was not only loss of woodland cover that brought about the decline of the red squirrel. It was largely viewed as a controversial animal, one that damaged forestry, and as such, a varmint to be eradicated at all costs. Coming from the species that invented clearfell with all its subsequent devastation, this is a sad irony. Squirrels were also wrongly blamed for killing songsters in large numbers. Squirrel hunting became commonplace with hunts set up all around the country. Feast days and Saints' Days - St Andrew's Day, Boxing Day, and even Christmas Day, were occasions for squirrel massacre as parties of keen hunters took to the woods armed with sticks and poles, beating dreys until the terrified occupants fled in a flurry. Like the trees, the squirrels were felled – but in this case the culprits wielded catapults, stones, or guns, instead of axes or chainsaws.

In the early 1900s, numerous squirrels were being culled. So-called 'vermin' returns from Cawdor Estate, near Inverness, document an astonishing 14,000 red squirrels killed over a 17-year period at a time when a bounty was paid for each squirrel's tail; all due to the threat the hapless creatures were said to pose to forestry. Some entrepreneurial keepers are rumoured to have cut off tails, and released squirrels in the belief that they would grow another, and thus they might be paid twice. Atholl Estates in Perthshire had similar records, and between 1891-1903, no less than 3,069 squirrels were accounted for, whilst the Glasgow Herald reported that the Ross-shire Squirrel Club killed 3,988 squirrels in 1904, and 4,727 the previous year.

"A society grows great when old men plant trees whose shade they know they shall never sit in."

*Greek Proverb*

# Reintroductions

It is hard to imagine that for centuries red squirrels were so heavily persecuted in this country, as indeed elsewhere in Europe, where their fur – sometimes referred to as vair – was used to line exotic garments.

They might also be caught in live traps and sent to markets further afield, sold as curiosities or cage pets. Most did not survive. Stress is one of a squirrel's greatest enemies. Then conversely – as deforestation and several severe winters led to their near total loss in the 18th century – a few enlightened landowners changed tack altogether and reintroduced red squirrels to some of their previous haunts. One of few places where a small population survived was at Rothiemurchus, in the Cairngorms, appropriately home now to the very squirrels that Neil knows and loves so well. Around the late 1700s, the Duchess of Buccleuch, and the Duke of Atholl, brought in squirrels from Scandinavia. These new arrivals successfully helped to re-colonise both the eastern and southern Highlands. A little later, in the mid-1800s, Lady Lovat had the foresight to bring stock into Argyllshire, and there were other landowners who saw fit to bring in new red squirrels to help boost the flagging population.

We have these forward-thinking souls to thank – for had this not been the case, then it is highly likely that the red squirrel would have been wiped out as a British species, and unceremoniously added to the list of extinctions.

# Famous squirrels

In 1903, Beatrix Potter put a delightful but naughty little red squirrel firmly on the map with the publication of The Tale of Squirrel Nutkin, a story that has enchanted generations of children and their parents ever since. This was an important turning point and raised the profile of the red squirrel considerably. Yet when the book was first published, squirrel hunting was still to the fore.

Some 50 years later, a red squirrel named Tufty would become the figurehead for a highly effective road safety campaign aimed at young children. When the Tufty Club was born, its badge portraying a cheery red squirrel was proudly worn by children all over the country. When I was four years old, my uncle gave me membership for a Christmas present, and I too wore my badge with pride.

Red squirrels have been through good and bad. Now it is rare to hear anyone say a detrimental word about an animal that is viewed as a national treasure, valued as a vital part of our ecosystems, as well as one of the country's most fascinating mammals. Attitudes have finally changed.

# A grey area

The landowners who first brought the larger, more dominant North American grey squirrel to the British Isles can have had little idea as to the damage and misery this wanton fad would cause. It was in 1876 that T.V. Brocklehurst first released grey squirrels to an estate in Cheshire. It is possible that they had been imported even earlier, though that remains a subject for conjecture. Soon the growing fashion for importing grey squirrels brought a further rash of introductions, and the stage was set for the opportunist grey to spread across the countryside at an alarming rate.

In Scotland, grey squirrels first put in an appearance in 1892, when G.S. Page of New Jersey brought some to Finnart on Loch Long in Dumbartonshire, where they began an impressively swift colonisation of the surrounding area. During the ensuing quarter of a century they spread out over a 300-mile radius. There were also several other Scottish introductions, including to Edinburgh Zoo in 1913. Some of the zoo animals escaped, and one imagines that the grey squirrels that still dominate Edinburgh's parks and gardens today are their distant cousins.

It quickly became apparent that in areas where the grey was establishing, the resident red squirrel population was beginning to struggle, retreating as its numbers fell dramatically. Greys were initially blamed for killing their smaller, prettier relations. However, this was not in fact the case – and the situation has turned out to be far more complex, and is still not wholly understood.

What is clear, however, is that the grey squirrel is a robust rodent. It is also destructive in young plantations. It is able to consume many natural foods long before they are ripe enough for the red squirrel to digest – acorns being a prime example. Greys are able to survive entirely in some deciduous woodland where often there is simply not enough food for reds. It is obvious that in an area where food is limited, the larger, more adaptable creature will always come out on top. This appears to be part of the issue with the presence of the grey squirrel in woods where the red squirrel previously thrived.

The fact that the grey squirrel also carries a lethal parapox virus with similar symptoms to myxomatosis in rabbits, and can pass this onto the vulnerable red squirrel, has long been of major concern. Whilst the grey squirrel is largely unaffected by the disease, once transmitted it proves fatal to a red. Death usually occurs in less than a fortnight.

As the dreadful truth of having an alien species in our midst unravelled, a new war began in an endeavour to eradicate the British countryside of another of man's foolish follies. In many areas – particularly in hotspots for red squirrels – greys are live trapped and humanely dispatched. This is not to everyone's liking; and where the grey is the only resident squirrel, there has been uproar. It is likely that we will never be totally free of the grey in this country. It is, however, illegal to release a grey squirrel, including those picked up perhaps when orphaned or injured. Some say that we must now accept the species as part of our ecosystem, similarly to the current situation with ring-necked parakeets that have become a dominant species in most London parks. However, for the red squirrel living in Caledonian pine forests, and healthy mixed woodlands in their strongholds such as Speyside, Perthshire, Angus, Aberdeenshire, Argyllshire, and Dumfries and Galloway, keeping the grey out is of the utmost importance.

# Drey-to-drey living

From an early age a squirrel instinctively makes its own drey. It may choose a wide range of trees, and sometimes uses a hollow, or old vacated woodpecker hole, or the fork of a large mature tree. In ancient broadleaved woodland there is plenty of choice. Generally, dreys are situated high up, sheltered from prevailing winds. However, in coniferous forest there is less choice of species, and it is also far harder to see dreys. In young woodland, it may be necessary to build in small spindly trees. The end result sometimes seems to dangle conspicuously like a weaverbird's nest in an African thorn tree, yet may be surprisingly secure. Summer dreys – often merely used for a passing snooze – are not as well built as those used for breeding and for winter dwelling. A primary drey has to be strong as well as perfectly insulated, for it must keep its occupants warm and dry. Sticks and leaves are woven together, and the interior densely lined with moss and lichen, sometimes bark strippings, dried grasses, feathers, foliage, and often copious amounts of sheep's wool, or other animal fibres.

One fallen drey that I found in hazel woods close to my home, was not only still jumping with fleas – indicating that it had recently been in use – but it was also lined with horse hair gathered from the adjacent field. I have found dreys richly lined with soft pigeon breast feathers perhaps plucked from a carcase, or collected from a sparrowhawk's plucking post. Squirrels are innovative.

Though squirrels seem antisocial with one another around the woodland, they will usually share a drey, particularly in winter when several will curl up entwined together for warmth. Most squirrels have several dreys in use at the same time, and move around between them. Not only does this minimise infestation with parasites, but it also gives the squirrel an alternative refuge when disturbed, or in the case where a drey has tumbled out of a tree in high winds. In such circumstances a lactating mother may move her young to safety, quickly re-establishing them in a new nursery.

A wide range of materials can be used to build and line a squirrel drey.

# The Curious Garden Squirrel

With our house surrounded by perfect red squirrel habitat, it's little wonder they are daily visitors to the garden. At almost any time during the day, you can look out of the window and somewhere in view there will likely be a squirrel up to some mischief or other. This is not unique to our house by any means – and in fact red squirrels are regular garden visitors wherever there is good habitat nearby.

The lichen-covered picket fence that runs around our house is a popular route for squirrels as they make their way to and from the woods. I knew that if I could get a picture of a squirrel taking this daily path with the cottage in the background, it would tell a nice story.

A remote camera was duly set in position and I took my place back in the house with the infrared trigger (I'm at the window behind the squirrel's head). As I reflected on the merits of a job that allowed me to sit in a nice comfy chair drinking tea and taking pictures, a squirrel appeared. Almost choking on my chocolate digestive, I grabbed the remote trigger and watched eagerly as it made its way along the fence like a tightrope walker. I fired a sequence of frames as it passed the camera – but a few metres on, it turned around, having realised there was something alien on its route. Tentatively, the squirrel came back towards the camera, clearly curious about this strange new object.

Sitting at the window I couldn't help but chuckle as the squirrel investigated this curious piece of Japanese technology. It struck the perfect pose that you see in this picture – just a frame before it jumped across onto the camera itself, to give it a proper examination.

I'd set out to capture a squirrel running along the fence – but in the end, fortune was on my side and this works so much better. What it is to have such obliging neighbours!

# What's on the menu?

The greatest part of a squirrel's life is spent frenetically searching for food. Squirrels are adaptable when it comes to finding sustenance, but cannot endure for long periods without a meal. As their energetic behaviour would suggest, they have a fast metabolism and burn energy quickly.

Though the small seeds found inside cones such as Scots pine and Norway spruce are a favoured part of the diet, their food varies greatly depending on seasonal availability. In spring, buds and sap from a wide variety of trees are important, and hazel catkins, the tender shoots of fruit trees, flowers, pollen, and lichen add to the diet. Bark is expertly stripped to reveal sugary sap beneath, and later in the season an assortment of fungi is collected and stored, and often left out to dry, wedged into the fissured bark of tree trunks, or taken to the drey to be consumed during hard times ahead. In gardens, squirrels may dig up various bulbs and nibble at them too. Squirrels drink from dewponds, water-filled leaves, and water that collects in tree cavities, as well as from burns and streams.

Though winters may be long and hard, it is perhaps surprising that summer is a lean period for a squirrel too when trees are in full leaf, and fruits, hazel nuts and acorns are not yet ready, and berries such as hawthorn are still to ripen.

# Vital protein

It is important to remember that the red squirrel is an omnivorous rodent and therefore takes advantage of a wide variety of food. During the summer when food is scarce, as it races through the canopy, a squirrel may encounter an unguarded nest. Both eggs and hatchlings can provide vital protein at a time when it is much needed. However, the small numbers of fledglings accounted for by squirrels does nothing to dent the avian population. Just as a goshawk, buzzard, carrion crow, fox or pine marten may take a squirrel, a squirrel in turn may occasionally add the odd avian delicacy to its menu. Squirrels have also been seen feeding on carrion, though this is an infrequent occurrence. The enchanting elf-like red squirrel is a Jekyll and Hyde. Life in the wild is tough, and a squirrel – like every other creature – has to adapt in order to survive.

Red squirrels are expert climbers and a scattering of stripped Scots pine cones is a sure sign of feeding high above in the canopy.

# Noisy eaters

S quirrels are noisy eaters. Stand in silence on a still day in a wood frequented by squirrels and you might hear nibbling noises coming from above, even if the squirrel remains elusive. I love to do this, particularly in high summer when the birds are in heavy moult and have grown silent, and the forest seems drowsy. Sometimes it can take a great deal of scanning, neck craned awkwardly, whilst peering into the verdant jungle above to find the source of the sound. And then there it is, a little rounded shape sitting aloft a branch high in the canopy chucking down unwanted bits as it feeds. Though equipped with massively strong nutcracker teeth that grow continuously, and are constantly worn down, extricating the seeds from inside hard pine and spruce cones requires immense skill. A cone is expertly turned around, often at speed, whilst being held tightly in the front paws, amid much loud munching. It is in this pose – whilst sitting upright with its tail held over its back – that we find the squirrel even more endearing. It seems almost human as its nimble paws with their sharp claws work just like human hands.

"We abuse land because we regard it as a commodity belonging to us. When we see land as a community to which we belong, we may begin to use it with love and respect."

*Aldo Leopold*

# Hide and seek

As the long days of summer fade, migrants depart; swallows and martins gather on wires, their dark shapes against the sky resembling minims and quavers on a music sheet. Soon they too will be gone. Now the woodland habitat begins to yield a rich harvest. Large flocks of winter thrushes, fieldfares and redwings descend from the north. As autumn approaches there is a bounteous glut, and a squirrel becomes ever more frenetic. It dashes back and forth collecting hazel nuts, beech masts, or ripe acorns, burying its finds in the woodland floor. This accelerated behaviour is indeed a race against time. It is as if every squirrel is in a rush, scurrying back and forth with much tail flicking – signalling to others to keep out of the way, and certainly not to interfere whilst they are so employed. Noses and front paws are often speckled brown with dark leaf litter and soil.

In our garden, the vegetable patch becomes a burial site, our tubs of plants also used to hide treasure. Crab apples and other orchard fruits are now ripe and may sustain the squirrels whilst the burying phase of their lives is at a peak, for their busyness uses much energy. However, peanuts in specialist feeders are seldom cached, and would rot before they were rediscovered. Autumn caches are a vital part of winter survival, and though a squirrel may take food buried by another, the outcome is the same. In oak woods, jays also bury thousands of acorns each autumn. Caches are often raided by wood mice and voles, but burying plenty ensures there is usually enough – and is also a part of natural regeneration, as forgotten acorns and hazelnuts eventually sprout, to become part of the forest of the future.

Against the backdrop of a snowy pinewood, a lone squirrel adopts a typical pose whilst pondering its next move.

# Up with the lark

Squirrels are early risers. They do not hibernate but may spend longer in their dreys during extremes of weather. They need to eat on a regular basis, and unlike hedgehogs that do hibernate, cannot go for long periods without food. In winter, they are abroad as soon as it is light, but in spring and summer, they are active well before dawn, and usually sleep for long periods in the middle of the day, taking summer siestas after their early start. They re-emerge in late afternoon for another frantic round of feeding around teatime. They are much harder to see when trees are in full leaf; when the days seem eternal they spend more time high in the drifting green awning.

# Nature's mineral boost

Deer shed their antlers annually. Roe bucks lose theirs between October and December, and grow new ones over the winter months, whilst red deer stags shed theirs in March and April. The larger the animal, the earlier it will cast its antlers. Often deer chew on a fallen antler for it provides an important source of calcium and phosphorus, and in the case of the red deer hind, may be a vital boost for her growing foetus at a lean time when it is much needed in spring. Squirrels are attracted to discarded antlers, and soon the signs of their sharp teeth marks indicate that they also take advantage of them to provide vital minerals. We leave an antler out for the squirrels that visit our garden, and usually fix it down placed in an upright position, so that it cannot be dragged away. Like this, it provides us with a great deal of entertainment. Squirrels of all ages are instantly drawn to it, and soon leave new tooth marks of their own. Youngsters play tig around the antler too, and climb up to its top, perching precariously like priceless pixies teetering to retain their balance. In some gardens kindly benefactors put out mineral-rich cuttlefish for their squirrels; these too are relished.

# Coat of many colours

Watching the resident squirrels in the woods around my home, it is easy to see that they vary in colour considerably. In a garden setting where many of the same animals appear daily, recognising individuals is also possible as variation between them becomes ever more apparent.

'How can you tell the difference between them?' is a question I am frequently asked. We have dark, auburn red squirrels, and some with streaks of tawny, russet, amber and gold through their pelts, and many variations in between. Some seem to have henna highlights in their glossy summer coats, whilst it is as if others have had a go at the bottle of peroxide to attain fashionable blonde highlights. Occasionally someone may send me an image of a pure blonde, or even an albino squirrel that is visiting a garden on a regular basis.

Tails reveal much too, and can have great colour variation. In 1905, the painter and naturalist John Everett Millais noted: 'From autumn to March their tails bleach, becoming cream or even white'. One of our visitors has a very dark tail, whilst another has a pale tail that is half the length it should be. The latter, a female, has been coming to the garden now for three years, and survives perfectly well with only half her tail. How she lost it is the subject of debate. Could she have had a narrow escape with a cat, dog or bird of prey? Or perhaps it was caught in a fence and broke off. When she first appeared it was perfectly healed with no sign of an open wound.

During the summer months, red squirrels lose their characteristic ear tufts and many sport a streamlined blond tail, which returns to the more familiar rufous colouration in autumn.

With regard to colouration, red squirrels in other parts of Europe also have a wide variation in hues. There are numerous sub-species of red squirrel, all of which freely interbreed. There is a school of thought that during the time that different red squirrels were introduced to this country, colour variation became more commonplace. Red squirrels from Europe and elsewhere were also frequently sold in London markets. Doubtlessly there were escapes, since a squirrel (competing closely with a badger) is the true Houdini of the British wild animal kingdom. Could this be the reason for such a wide variation? As a wildlife rehabilitator, I receive many injured tawny owls that also vary greatly in colour from the richly red-rufous phase, to grey-phase birds. Buzzards may have similar variation. From a naturalist's point of view, I am inclined to think that – like humans – all red squirrels are individuals. After all, nature does not regiment anything.

# Summer Squirrel

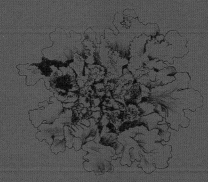

Capturing that special look when a squirrel reveals something of its character is never easy, and not something you can engineer. All I can do as a photographer is to be prepared and to make sure I make the most of those split-second opportunities.

For the past couple of years there has been a petite female squirrel living in the pinewood close to my home. Although every squirrel is an individual with a distinctive personality, now and again one stands out – and this little female has become a real character.

Settled next to the base of a tall pine with my camera at the ready, it was now a matter of waiting. An hour passed and I had a brief visit from a squirrel – but it wasn't the one I was after.

As time ticked away, I listened to the birds in the forest canopy before dozing off in the warmth of the morning sun. I don't know how long I'd been snoozing when suddenly I became conscious of something watching me. I looked up, still groggy – and there was the small female just six metres away, clinging to the side of a huge pine and peering at me intently. Still half asleep – so much for being ready – I turned the camera in her direction and through the long lens I could see her every detail, including clear signs that she was feeding kits.

It was the pose and her lovely expression, however, that really caught my attention. She had that perfect look – that cheeky, inquisitive, alert look – that said so much about her as an individual animal.

She had important motherly work to do, of course, and as she went off on her way, I wondered how long she'd been watching me, and what else she'd been up to whilst I dozed. There are always surprises with red squirrels.

*Neil*

WOODLAND TALES

# A question of sex

A nother question I am often asked is 'how do you tell the sexes apart?' That too is fairly simple, particularly when a feeding squirrel sits up with food in front paws and reveals a little more of its anatomy. However, there is no obvious size difference between the sexes. Lactating females are quite obvious, and their four pairs of teats often visible. When they are engorged it indicates that they have a growing nest of young. Full mammary glands sometimes make the squirrel appear fat which will be far from the case. At this time a female needs to feed often to ensure she has enough milk. It is always exciting to see these animals; the arrival of their young in the garden is eagerly anticipated.

# Antics with youngsters

Though we know that a particular female is suckling young in a nearby drey, there may be a long wait before the new offspring appear. When they do, the other antisocial squirrels in the vicinity chase them furiously. To begin with their large hind feet are particularly apparent, and they have wonderfully long feathery ear tufts, that make them stand out from the bossy adults.

Youngsters can be slow to familiarise themselves with the layout of the feeders. Learning to open them can be a real puzzle. They can see the nuts inside but have no idea how to lift the lid. To assist, I prop them open and watch to see what happens next. Even then they may choose the bird peanut feeders at first, and nibble nuts through the mesh instead of opening the easily-accessible box feeders. Once they have learnt, they often get right inside, and the lid drops down whilst they are nibbling happily. When an adult comes along, and pushes the lid open, there is a mad explosion, a champagne bottle after a good shake – two effervescent squirrels flying into the air in a russet spray of surprise and excitement, ending in a mad chase through the trees. Young squirrels are incredibly playful and their antics hilarious. Life is never dull when there are squirrels around.

Exploring a daunting world.

# Keeping up to scratch

During the spring, a squirrel can look very shabby. Often, after more time spent in the drey, parasites take hold; mites, fleas and lice are just a handful of the afflictions that are faced by squirrels, and there may be considerable scratching as well as hair loss, exacerbated by a heavy moult. During the spring, I have noted that our squirrels appear to lose their coats from the front to the back, whilst it is the reverse in the autumn. In spring, adults lose their fabulous ear tufts too. This may temporarily alter their appearance, and the little faces become rather ratty.

Sometimes the moult is drastic, the unfortunate squirrels left with large unsightly bald patches. I sometimes receive calls from concerned people asking what can be done to help. Unfortunately there is little that can be done. However, other mammals and birds are also afflicted with the same problem. Note a male blackbird in spring when he is in all his finery, plumage glossed with black varnish, dapper, not a feather out of place, singing his heart out, and filling the garden with his finest arias. By mid-summer he too looks shabby, exhausted from the demands of rearing several broods of young. He is balding, his sheen is gone, and he is in heavy moult, keeping a low profile almost as if ashamed. And when roe and red deer go through their moult, they can often resemble an old charity shop fur coat that has been attacked by moths. Moulting is a necessary process, and few creatures look their best at this time – least of all a squirrel.

"If a man walks in the woods for the love of them half of each day, he is in danger of being regarded as a loafer. But if he spends his days as a speculator, shearing off those woods and making the earth bald before her time, he is deemed an industrious and enterprising citizen."

*Henry David Thoreau*

# Tales of tails

A red squirrel's tail is one of its finest assets. Beatrix Potter cleverly painted Squirrel Nutkin and his fellow squirrels sailing over to Owl Island using their tails as sails – a charming picture that has been etched in my psyche ever since, but it's not perhaps strictly accurate. However, a squirrel does make a great deal of use of its tail. It can be used as an umbrella, a parasol, and a windbreak – so why not a sail? It may be used as a rudder, or almost as a steering wheel, helping with balance as the squirrel dances fast through the treetops. It can aid its owner with precision during expansive leaps of faith through dense tangles of branches. The tail is also frequently used as a blanket or muffler on cold days whilst snoozing in an exposed spot, or when inside the drey.

Perhaps one of its most important uses is as a flag. A squirrel uses its tail to signal, waving it in greeting or warning, informing other squirrels of its mood, and frequently informing them to steer clear. It will also crossly wave its tail as it peers down on a person below. Sometimes when I am filling up an empty feeder, one of our little squirrels will bravely sit quite close and chatter, and wave its tail at me, in clear displeasure. After all I am late and should have filled up the feeder before it ran out. Whilst walking in woods with my three collies far from the resident garden squirrels that have grown accustomed to me, we often stop to watch a squirrel high above us, and it too will wave its tail crossly – warning us to keep away. For a squirrel, its tail is a vital means of expression, and as such reveals much about its humour and disposition.

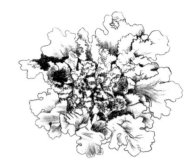

# Matters of a sexual nature

A squirrel becomes sexually mature at about a year old. However, this will be largely dependent on food availability for it will not breed if it is in poor body condition. Mating can take place throughout the year but there are two peaks, one early in the season, and one in summer. When well-nourished it is quite usual for a female to give birth to two litters of kits. I have received orphan squirrels with their eyes still shut in early March, and once was brought a fallen drey in mid-February containing five dead young, still naked and blind, and possibly only about two days old.

The gestation period is approximately 38 days. Most spring litters are born in March and April, with subsequent litters born later in the summer – though there are exceptions, and litters have been recorded in January in parts of England.

A squirrel's courtship is like its eating habits – noisy. Pairs are not loyal to one another, and do not forge a bond at any stage other than to mate. To begin with, the female he pursues will scold an approaching male, and the pair chatter and chitter to one another as if thoroughly irritated. Then a frenetic chase begins as they fly round and round a tree trunk, mad whirling dervishes, flurries of red jinking giddily, the sound of sharp little claws clutching bark, and the atmosphere scattered with flaky bark dust and lichen. It's a fascinating scene, and I frequently find myself glued as another mating ritual begins. Often a second, and even a third male may appear and the chase becomes ever more spectacular till I have no idea which squirrel is which any more. Sometimes this may continue for days until one male is successful. The only time I have witnessed squirrels grooming one another is after mating. Then all is calm as they melt back into the treetops, and the female will not usually accept further advances from other males until the next time she is in oestrus.

# The rearing of young

After mating, the male squirrel has nothing further to do with the rearing of his offspring. He may mate with several other females throughout the year. Meanwhile, the female begins either to upgrade a drey she already uses, or to build herself an entirely new one, taking great care to line it meticulously with soft warm material. She may have up to six kits, although three to five is average. They are born naked, blind and defenceless, and at this stage the mother will not venture far as they are vulnerable, and require her rich milk at regular intervals. They do not open their eyes until they are about three weeks of age. Now they are covered in velvety ginger fur, and their long previously hirsute tails begin to look like that of a squirrel, and less like that of a rat. At this stage the extraordinary large hind feet with their double-jointed ankles seem far too big for the babies; it is as if they have not yet fully grown into them. Claws are also well developed from an early age, to enable the inexperienced youngsters to retain a steadfast grip as they emerge from the drey at around two months old. Babies are suckled for approximately 10 weeks, and it is at this stage that the female's nipples become even more visible as the fast-growing youngsters tug competitively at their long-suffering mother. Once suckling stops, the female will regain her svelte shape almost immediately.

Young squirrels may be seen playing in close proximity to their drey – though with dense leaf cover a good view is not guaranteed. They must soon leave and build their own dreys, and run the gauntlet of the resident squirrels. Frequently chased and hounded out, they may eventually move further afield to establish new territories of their own.

# Young squirrels - hard times ahead

Once weaned and outside the safety of the natal drey, baby squirrels have quickly to become independent. They frequently struggle to find enough food, and may succumb to starvation. Summer's torrential deluges can lead to animals becoming chilled if dreys built by inexperienced juveniles do not offer sufficient protection. Young squirrels have thicker summer pelts to help protect them from the vagaries of the climate, but even this is not always sufficient to guard against exposure. Youngsters in prime habitat or that visit garden feeders have a far better chance of survival – and as more people put out suitable food, this lifeline may greatly raise chances of living through the first winter. Mortality rate at this time is high.

# Island living

The only Scottish island that currently has a population of red squirrels is Arran. They were introduced during the 1950s, and have since thrived. One of the benefits to island living is that it is far easier to keep the invasive grey squirrel at bay, and – as on the Isle of Wight in England – the reds are able to thrive without competition from the larger squirrel. It is unlikely that historically there were ever red squirrels on any Hebridean Islands, nor indeed in Orkney and Shetland – trees won't thrive in winds of frequent hurricane force. However, though they have never been present, perhaps specific forested areas of Mull and Islay could sustain small squirrel populations in the future.

# Autumn Encounter

Autumn is a magical season and my favourite time of the year. I suspect the squirrels might agree, as this is a time of plenty with a wide range of natural food available. With such a rich palette of russet colours in the beech and oak woods next to my home and the squirrels as busy as ever, I wanted to make the most of this brief window of opportunity. Such intensity of colour can be all too fleeting as high winds can strip the trees bare in a single night.

A real sense of anticipation gripped me as I took the short walk from my house to the woods. The light was perfect. On my approach I could already see a couple of squirrels foraging on the ground where I put out their daily snacks.

Normally I place my camera where I intend to position myself, and then go round placing the food on the spots where I want the squirrels to go – but for some reason, on this occasion I had the camera slung casually over my shoulder as I went about dispensing the food. As I reached the bottom of one of the old oaks, I heard the distinctive chitter of a squirrel in the tree above me. I looked up and there was one of the squirrels peeping around the lichen-covered oak against a backdrop of glorious autumn foliage. Perfect!

This was one of those moments that wildlife photographers yearn for. Praying that the squirrel wouldn't move I eased the camera from my shoulder and pointed it skywards. Still the curious squirrel looked down at me – no doubt wondering, not for the first time, what I was up to. I took a quick shot in case it fled, then quickly readjusted some settings before taking several more frames. I had captured the shot I'd had in my mind's eye since last autumn.

Temptation quickly got the better of the squirrel and he started to make his way down the tree to reach his well-earned nut. How I would have cursed if I had stuck to my normal routine, and had the camera set-up as usual. Luck – as well as light – plays such a vital role in a nature photographer's world.

*Neil*

WOODLAND TALES

# Squirrels on the move

Work continues to move a few squirrels from areas where they are plentiful into suitable habitat that they could not otherwise reach naturally due to its isolation, for squirrels do not like travelling over open ground. Carried out under licence from Scottish Natural Heritage, this specialist work is closely monitored at all stages. Prospective areas are rigorously surveyed before any decisions are taken to ensure that the habitat can adequately sustain its new residents. So far it has proved highly efficacious.

In the 1980s, Alan Watson Featherstone realised that the ancient Caledonian Forest – that had once covered the majority of the Scottish Highlands – was at risk of disappearing completely. He recognised that most of the remnants of pine forest were largely composed of old trees, nearing the end of their life, and began an ambitious mission to save them by creating the charity Trees for Life. And since 1989, it has been doing just that.

Trees for Life propagates and plants thousands of native trees annually – including Scots pine, aspen, rowan, oak, willow, alder and juniper. Individuals as well as communities have become involved and thousands of volunteers have helped to plant around 1.3 million trees to date, and thousands more trees are able to seed and grow naturally, protected from deer grazing by fencing.

Autumn in Glen Affric where Trees for Life have been regenerating the wildwood for 25 years.

In 2015, Trees for Life started a programme to help red squirrels, creating new populations by reintroducing them to their former strongholds. The project builds on three successful reintroductions pioneered by Roy Dennis of the Highland Foundation for Wildlife.

Squirrels are caught at sites across Highland and Moray, where populations flourish, and given a health check before being carefully transported to release sites in specially-made nest boxes. Only small numbers are taken from any one location to ensure no negative impact on existing populations. The charity provides food for a few months after the release to help the squirrels settle easily into their new surroundings, and the populations are then monitored for signs of breeding and to check how they are spreading throughout the new habitat.

This work is a hugely positive step for red squirrel conservation. As well as increasing both their numbers and the area inhabited by them, it is – critically – being carried out in a region that is totally free from grey squirrels. The importance of this cannot be understated – the new populations will flourish as they once did without risk of competition, or from the dreaded, fatal squirrel pox.

It's not only red squirrels that benefit. The project offers a unique route for local communities to become involved in wildlife conservation, with residents assisting in all aspects of the reintroductions – from releasing the squirrels, to helping with their subsequent feeding and monitoring.

As of December 2016, 55 red squirrels have been reintroduced to two locations in northwest Scotland. Young squirrels born at the release sites have been regularly spotted and – with another six translocations planned over the next two years – there is once again real hope for the red squirrel and its secure future in the forest.

Becky Priestley, Wildlife Officer with Trees for Life, tempts red squirrels into the translocation traps with a handful of peanuts.

# Squirrel viewing

Estimates of current UK red squirrel numbers stand at around 160,000, though it could be far lower. Some 75 per cent of this figure is accounted for in Scotland, with small populations clinging onto a few isolated areas in England and Wales. The Lake District, Isle of Wight, and Brownsea Island are excellent places to see red squirrels in England, whilst they thrive on Anglesey in northwest Wales. Many tourists visiting Scotland for the first time have red squirrels firmly on their list of things to see. They are as highly ranked as golden eagles and otters – further evidence of the love we now have for this delightful mammal. For many years I worked as a wildlife guide and was constantly surprised by the numbers of visitors who had only ever seen a grey squirrel. Almost 20 years ago, red squirrels were often hard to find even in much of Perthshire, but today numbers appear to be rising steadily, and happily sightings – though never guaranteed – are becoming more commonplace. Increase of good habitat, and the continuous removal of grey squirrels has paid off.

# Perils

A red squirrel is as perfectly adapted to its life in trees as a wild goat is to its life on vertiginous, craggy cliff faces. It can cling, grip, run, leap, and almost fly through its sylvan surroundings with the ease of a knife through soft butter, and it is also an excellent swimmer, though would not take to water through choice. But on the ground it can be vulnerable and often seems far from streetwise, even slightly slow and clumsy. Young squirrels all too often end their days in the jaws of the domestic dog or cat – just one of many reasons why in our garden, we choose not to familiarise our small visitors by hand-feeding them. If only cat owners would fit their pets with elasticated collars with loud bells attached, a great many accidental deaths could be averted. Roads are of course one of a squirrel's biggest hazards, as indeed they are for humans. Many inexperienced juvenile squirrels in particular are killed in summer – and though in more built-up areas feeding squirrels can make all the difference to their survival, where gardens are adjacent to roads this may carry a high price. The average lifespan of a wild squirrel is two to five years, though in captivity it may live for at least ten.

# Pine marten versus red squirrel

In recent years, the return of the pine marten to many of its previous haunts has been the subject of controversy. Those who dislike this beautiful arboreal opportunist are quick to blame it for killing red squirrels. However, in a healthy balanced ecosystem the two species should be well able to survive alongside one another. Recent research has shown that the omnivorous pine marten appears to prefer hunting the slower, heavier, less agile grey squirrel. Indeed, it is thought that where this happens, the red squirrel thrives. Due to this, the pine marten has finally been exonerated. It would be unrealistic not to accept that from time to time an unwary red squirrel may be added to the pine marten's fare, whilst equally a pine marten may end up as fare for a golden eagle, or other large raptor. Nature retains a balance, but sadly we have thrown that out of kilter.

# Names, nonsense & collective nouns

Considering the wealth of nouns that can be used to describe the cheery disposition, antics and character of the gorgeous red squirrel, its collective nouns are disappointing. The only two in regular use are a drey, and a scurry, the latter being far more descriptive. Having seen young squirrels fast asleep together entwined, entangled and in a rusty heap so dense that it is hard to ascertain which body, tail, head and foot belongs to which animal, a tangle, knot, hotchpotch, or hugger-mugger would seem more apt. Whilst to describe their behaviour, a capriciousness, an exhilaration, a sprightliness, or perhaps a mischief would be more endearing.

A red squirrel's Latin name, Sciuris vulgaris, also seems inappropriate since there is nothing vulgar about this little animal. The name squirrel has ancient, possibly Greek origins, stemming from a word meaning 'shade tail' – further evidence of a squirrel using its tail as a parasol.

The red squirrel's Gaelic names are, feòrag, and toghmall, whilst the French call it écureuil, and the Germans, Eichhörnchen – literally meaning 'oak kitten', a name that aptly depicts its spirited disposition. The name squirrel can equally be applied to a person who hoards or collects items. This is reference to the animal's habit of burying its food for winter. It appears that the red squirrel garnered far more country nicknames south of the border than in Scotland, where it was sometimes called con. These include: squaggy, puggy, scropel and scraggy. None are appropriately flattering.

"People who will not sustain
trees will soon live in a world
that cannot sustain people."

*Bryce Nelson*

# Uses for a squirrel

I t's still possible to buy paint brushes made of pure squirrel hair taken from their tails. These are favoured by artists the world over, and used for fine detail. Though some restaurants, and indeed individuals, put the unfortunate grey squirrel on the menu, it is a long time since red squirrel was regularly eaten. Both types are said to taste like rabbit. I have only once sampled a small piece of marinated grey squirrel, and I am not sure I would repeat it. And I am certainly relieved that the days of eating red are long gone. Garments made of squirrel pelt are also relegated to the distant past.

# Close encounters

Being brought a drey containing live baby squirrels is a great privilege, but with it comes a weighty responsibility. When I have a call to inform me a drey has blown down, and it contains young, I advise leaving it for a few hours untouched in the hope that the mother will return. When under threat, squirrels will often move their offspring to a new nursery. As this usually happens in severe weather, babies can quickly chill. Only if the mother does not return will I undertake the rearing of the unfortunate young. We are a poor substitute for an animal's parent.

Opening a drey is an extraordinary experience. Inside there may be kits perhaps only hours, or days old: naked, blind and helpless. Then their survival is dubious. Most of the young squirrels I have reared have been less than a fortnight old with their eyes still shut, but they have been covered in gingery velvet fur. Once at this stage, I know that they have had their mother's colostrum over their first 48 hours. This is vital to any animal's survival as colostrum contains irreplaceable antibodies. Now they stand a far better chance – though kits require a great deal of care, and must also be stimulated to pass waste matter, something carried out by their mother.

It's impractical to keep kits in their drey; I use a pure wool hat preferably shrunk in the washing machine. It resembles the felt-like mossy interior of a drey. The squirrels adapt well and disappear inside its cosy confines to slumber blissfully. They must be fed every few hours, including through the night, and are given kitten milk substitute in a syringe with a soft teat attached. The correct milk mixture is key to success – diarrhoea is one of the biggest killers of orphan mammals. Though the kits are often infested with fleas, using powder is not an option as they are already under stress; any noxious substance could tip the balance at this critical point.

On one occasion, having fed three tiny kits during the small hours, I returned to bed as silently as I could to avoid waking my partner Lomhair. I could hear his regular breathing beside me indicating he slept on regardless. After a few minutes I felt something tickling my hand, and gently touched it. Then it happened again, and again, and I slapped at it in desperation. A voice beside me suddenly asked, 'We are not alone, are we?' – and we leapt out of bed tugging back the sheets to find several tiny, erratically bouncing culprits. These however were not human fleas; the squirrel is their specialist host. It is unusual for them to hang around or bite. I never know where they go but we were not bothered further after this hilarious nocturnal encounter. Having fleas as bedfellows though is highly undesirable.

Once the squirrels have their eyes open the fun truly begins, for they become jack-in-the-boxes appearing cheekily from their woollen drey, and racing around their big wooden box where we put branches and logs for them to climb. After playing and feeding they collapse exhausted, vanish again, and are peaceful until it's time for the next meal. I wean them on a mixture of crushed digestive biscuit, nuts and seeds, grated apple or carrot, mixed with their milk, and they paddle in this sloppy mixture and plaster themselves in sticky mess like naughty children. Then they must be cleaned with warm, damp cotton wool, something they seem to enjoy. They squeak and chitter to one another gleefully as they erupt around the obstacles, manoeuvring with the skill and elasticity of Russian gymnasts. And then they crash and burn, and tumble back to bed.

Eventually they are so swift and active, tongues of flame impossible to control, escaping and leaping round the room, up the curtains, along the dresser. With such happy madness catching them is out of the question. Only exhaustion ends their mischief. Now they are ready to upsize to a large aviary lined with pine branches. Its floor is covered with deep leaves, cones, nuts, berries and seeds. At night they are moved outside in their sleeping box. Then all close contact is stopped, and I only go in to put out fresh food and water. It is surprising how quickly they become wary. They stay in the aviary for some weeks and must learn to open the nut feeder boxes prior to release. Their day of freedom brings not only a sense of delight for us, but also real anxiousness. It's a tough world out there, and they are vulnerable, and may disappear completely off the radar. Sometimes they return to the aviary and sleep in their box, and sometimes the resident squirrels go in to explore and pinch food. In a world where every red squirrel counts, we have done all we can and hopefully these youngsters thrive and spread new genes through the woodland.

# A Winter's Tale

WOODLAND TALES

Still half asleep I opened the curtains to reveal a winter wonderland with several inches of soft, powdery snow carpeting the woodland beyond the house. Snow can be a grind for many – but for photography it adds an enchanting element and, combined with the squirrels, it can be truly magical.

Within 20 minutes of getting up I was on my way down to the squirrels, taking in the wonder of the snow-covered forest, which now looked more like a scene from Narnia. As I reached the feeding site, I could see the squirrels had already visited – with tiny paw prints dotted across the carpet of white. One set of prints led up a nearby oak and I could see their owner half way up the tree waiting for my arrival.

With food secreted in a handful of spots, I settled in, waiting for what I thought must surely be an early appearance from the oak tree squirrel.  It sat and sat and then sat some more. After what seemed like an age, another squirrel caught my eye; it had sneaked in while I was pre-occupied and it was already tucking into a welcome hazelnut.

Turning my camera on the new visitor, a furious chittering from above suddenly erupted. It was clear that the squirrel up the tree had now noticed the intruder. Oblivious, the feeding squirrel finished its snack, whilst out of the corner of my eye I could see the previously apathetic squirrel now making its move. Like a miniature snowplough, it pushed the soft snow earthwards as it made its away along a thick bough. Realising the inevitable outcome, I focused on the squirrel at the foot of the tree and sure enough, it was duly snowballed from above.

I don't speak squirrel but I can imagine an expletive-laden exchange between the two. I'm not sure if it was my imagination but I thought I detected a positively smug look on the squirrel above as it looked down on its bedraggled neighbour. There is never a dull moment with these mischievous little creatures.

*Neil*

# The future pinewood

One particular wild place with a healthy population of red squirrels has been luring me enticingly for the past two decades. It's a work in progress abundant with life, bringing hope for other such woodland ventures. It is soon after dawn on a milky-grey spring morning as I take to the hill. Here deer fencing has been removed, for it has played its part enabling verdant natural regeneration to blossom on an ancient forest site.

Shafts of watery sunlight massage distant snow-stippled hills, gradually painting an ocean of dark pines with fleeting gold filaments. In a clearing of frosted tawny grasses, a primal ritual is taking place. Blackcock are on their lek, displaying immaculate blue-black plumage enhanced by engorged crimson wattles, as flashes of white under-feathers are revealed in a puff. They have been returning to this breeding ceremony arena for generations, to show off and compete with one another, backing and advancing in a series of choreographed manoeuvres. Their greyhens, high in a larch tree, feed on buds; plum pudding shapes against the pallor of daybreak. Like the blackgame, red squirrels are amorous too, chasing one another around a sun-tinted pine trunk temporarily glowing as orange-red as their pelts.

A male black grouse in full battle cry.

On the skyline a tree stands skeletal. The clean lines of a raven's dark silhouette broken only by wispy throat hackles as it calls with a harsh krrrk. Its mate will already be on eggs for this is a bird, like the golden eagle, and the crossbill, that usually nests early in the season. A curlew cries mournfully, adding grace notes to the distinctive bubbling sound of jousting blackcock. The wood is alive with orchestration.

Crested tits have survived the long, hard winter and prospect a fissured pine bole. Dependent on a myriad insects and seeds, they constantly search amongst the leaf litter, emitting their shrill zee, zee, zee calls. Parties of other tits and goldcrests may join them. Like the red squirrel, this rare member of the titmouse family stores food for the harsher months. Valuable invertebrate-rich dead wood bears the pockmarks of a great-spotted woodpecker's drilling. His rhythmic drumming echoes across the glen. Soon the cuckoo and willow warbler will arrive, adding new songs to the Scottish spring, and nesting golden plover will call plaintively from surrounding moorland. A buzzard mews. The blackcock will shortly retire, continuing their breeding dance once more at sundown.

Crested tit, another denizen of the pinewood, silhouetted against a winter sunset.

This pinewood is exemplary. Here our three native species of conifer, Scots pine, juniper and yew grow in profusion. Its open spaces are dappled with holly, rowan, ash, and bird cherry; the lower reaches by a burn fringed with contorted oak and hazel. There are dippers and tiny amber spotted trout. Willows and alders paddle in peaty pools where frogs come to spawn, and midges hatch forth in billions. As the days lengthen and the sun rises high in the sky, iridescent dragonflies will flit. Curious conical castles conceal colonies of large wood ants, their laborious work symbiotic to the health of the woodland. When dew is heavy, the understory of blaeberry, cowberry and heather is latticed with thousands of spiders' webs. In summer, foxgloves stand aloof, as the sun teases out nautilus shapes of gently unfurling ferns at their feet.

A sexton beetle, smart in black and orange, stops atop an emerald cushion of moss. Bees and hoverflies will hum lazily as the rare pink-white twinflower shyly shows its faces, with wintergreens, wood anemone, wood sorrel, and orchids: twayblade, and ladies' tresses. Mixed flocks of chaffinches and siskins chatter in the canopy. A pair of Scottish crossbills is caught in a sunbeam, the male's waistcoat flamboyantly blushing. These specialists, like the squirrels, are extraordinarily equipped to extricate the winged seeds from deep within tough pine cones, their crossed mandibles allowing them to scissor through to the heart of the matter.

Exposed roots are marked by pine marten scats; a badger has been excavating an anthill's sandy loam. The atmosphere is perfumed with earthiness and the pungency of fox. Sometimes in winter I find otter tracks on snowy paths by the burn's edge, or their sprint on rocks fringed in spring with primrose and celandine. During severe winter storms, mountain hares descend for shelter, amid brown hares, and roe and red deer. One winter, an area of mature pines was used as a roost by a juvenile golden eagle, and a sea eagle; their large elliptical pellets and white splats left as evidence on wind-scoured earth. There used to be wildcats here too, together with the great capercaillie, nicknamed horse of the woods. As this secret wood flourishes and continues its miraculous cycle of constant death and renewal from season to season, they could return.

This is the world the red squirrel needs, mixed woodland where nature takes precedence and is unmanaged – where nature manages nature in its own way, allowing an interdependent ecosystem to burgeon with life.

"When we try to pick out anything by itself, we find it hitched to everything else in the universe."

*John Muir*

# Sylvan pedestal

T he red squirrel is finally firmly on a sylvan pedestal where, with our concerted efforts, it must remain. It's hit the bottom but is now a golden flame of hope that must never be extinguished again. It does indeed have a healthy future if we can only help to restore its priceless habitat. There are few forests where man has not left his mark and intervened at some point. It is now timely for man to intervene once more. This is no short-term plan. We must think positively far into the future – our goal to re-establish the wildwood so that the red squirrel and the other magnificent creatures great and small that share its world may thrive in safety. If we can do this then, rest assured, Nature will do the rest.

# Thanks

Publishing this book was only possible through the incredible generosity of hundreds of backers who supported our crowdfunding campaign: thank you to you all.

The backers listed here went the extra mile and for that we would like to add an extra thank you.

## BRONZE LEVEL SUPPORTERS

| | |
|---|---|
| Julie Ellis | George N. Rutherford |
| Peter Barnes | M and C Dennys |
| Mark Green | Ann Cook |
| Richard Rees | Tanya Ware |
| Rob Stubbs | Innes MacNeill |
| Emma Baguley | Wendy Anderson |
| Nigel Teece | Callie Ullman |
| Craig MacInnes | Jane Hope |
| Peter Davison | Ann Wakeling |
| Cathy Fitzherbert | Wendy Salisbury |
| Jeanne T Spinks | Victoria Fraser |
| Ellie Rothnie | Shirley Nield |
| Terry Scroggie | Krisha Brandon |
| Isobel and Ian Short | |
| Ian and Debbie Johns | |
| Kenny White | |
| Ian Whinnett | |

## SILVER LEVEL SUPPORTERS

| | |
|---|---|
| Dr. Stefano Ragogna | Katrina Watson |
| Jonathan Piers Tyler | Maria Breas |
| Roger W Eads | Paul Barrow |
| Luke Sponholz | Jackie Walker |
| Alex Haggarty | Simon Whalley |
| Gordon Gray Stephens | Mairi Philp |
| Amy Reams | Steve and Karen Thomas |
| Anne Gray | Mad Grandma, Lucy, Scott, |
| Charles Galloway | Tone and Bad Lol |
| Andrew Gransden | Sandy Morrison |
| Clare Dyker | Robert A Greenwood |
| Jimmie and Rosie Reid | Linda Morley |
| Dave Cox | Mr Lawrence Smith |
| Steve Morris | Andrew Calderwood |
| Jamie Mina | Basil Groundsell and Wendy |
| Melanie Becker and | Collens |
| Sebastian Fröhlich | Dr Julie Hutson |

## GOLD LEVEL SUPPORTERS

Duncan Emsley

Rob Johnston

Jon Morris

Sir Cameron Mackintosh

The following organisations supported the funding in a variety of ways and deserve special mention.

Trees for Life

**www.treesforlife.org.uk**

Northshots Photo Adventures

**www.northshots.com**

Speyside Wildlife

**www.speysidewildlife.co.uk**

Wild Arena

**www.wildarena.com**

## PLATINUM LEVEL SUPPORTERS

The European Nature Trust

**www.theeuropeannaturetrust.com**

The European Nature Trust (TENT) supports and funds initiatives that preserve and restore wild habitats in Europe. The translocation of red squirrels to Alladale Wilderness Reserve and surrounding estates in Sutherland was a phenomenally successful project. Today, there are clear signs of a breeding population, as TENT continues to aid the expansion of red squirrels across their natural range.

# Acknowledgements

Without the support and belief from a great many people, this book would never have seen the light of day.

Firstly a massive thanks to everyone who backed the crowdfunding campaign. Your enthusiasm and support over that nerve-wracking November was just incredible and you made this book possible: hats off to you all.

I need to thank the team at SCOTLAND: The Big Picture for taking on the publishing of this book and never doubting they could make it real. Peter Cairns, Mark Hamblin, Emma Brown and James Shooter - thank you so much for the endless hours you have invested. Also, I appreciate the wonderful words from Polly Pullar; I can't think of anyone I'd have rather collaborated with.

Over many, many years the encouragement and support from my family and friends has been immense. From my mum and late father, my brother Alan, his wife Lynn and their children, Scott and Leanne, not to mention all my aunts, uncles and cousins: I cannot thank you enough.

I am blessed with some amazing friends who have always been there for me. Lisa Naylor, my squirrel buddy and friend, a sincere thank you for the many days we spent in the squirrel woods; we had some memorable times with those squirrels.

Several Highland estates have been very helpful over the years; in particular I would like to express my thanks to Kinrara Estate, Kinrara Estate Partnership and Rothiemurchus Estate.

My most heartfelt thank you goes to my partner and rock, Jackie. Without you I would be lost and words are not enough for the understanding and support you give me. I thank my lucky stars each and every day for having you in my life.

I have to mention my little red friends, who for the past two decades have brought me so much pleasure. You've made me laugh, cry and everything in between. Our journey together continues.

Finally, I would like to dedicate this book to my late father Torquil; I very much wish he was here to see it.

*Neil*

Neil McIntyre

Neil McIntyre is a professional nature photographer based in the Cairngorms National Park from where he runs his wildlife photography tours and image library. Apart from red squirrels, his work focuses on a wide range of species near his home, as well as throughout Scotland.

Neil's work is widely published and used in many national magazines and newspapers as well as by prominent conservation organisations. In addition, his images have featured in over 25 books. His work has been recognised in the prestigious BBC Wildlife Photographer of the Year and the British Wildlife Photography Awards.

**www.neilmcintyre.com**

Polly Pullar is a writer, photographer, wildlife rehabilitator and field naturalist, and claims that her deep passion for the natural world was fuelled by her childhood spent in Ardnamurchan. She is the wildlife writer for the Scottish Field, and contributes to the Scots Magazine and People's Friend every month, as well as to a wide range of other publications. She has written five books including, Rural Portraits – Scotland's Native Farm Animals, Characters & Landscapes, Fauna Scotica – Animals and People in Scotland, co-authored with Mary Low, and, A Drop in the Ocean – Lawrence MacEwen and the Island of Muck.

She lives in Highland Perthshire with a large menagerie that includes Shetland sheep, a red deer hind and three collies.

**www.pollypullar.com**